MW00522898

Medieval Queens

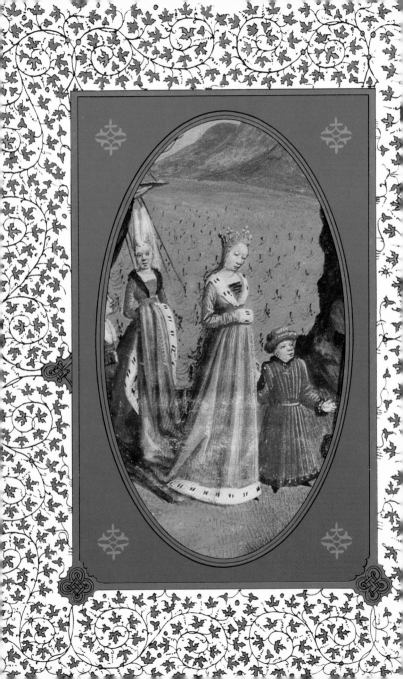

Medieval Queens

A PERPETUAL DAY BOOK

Clarkson N. Potter/Publishers

Copyright © 1990 by Garamond Publishers Limited

*All rights reserved. No part of this book may be
reproduced or transmitted in any form or by any
means, electronic or mechanical, including photocopying,
recording, or by any information storage and retrieval
system, without permission in writing from the publisher.*

*Published by Clarkson N. Potter, Inc., 201 East 50th
Street, New York, NY 10022. Originally published in
Great Britain by Garamond Publishers Limited in 1990.*

CLARKSON N. POTTER, POTTER, *and colophon are trademarks
of Clarkson N. Potter, Inc.*

Manufactured in Italy

Library of Congress Cataloging-in-Publication Data

Phillips, Phoebe.
    The medieval queens daybook: les très beaux jours / Phoebe
Phillips.
        p.   cm.
    ISBN 0-517-58056-X: $10.95
    1. Great Britain–Queens–Biography. 2. France–Queens–
Biography. 3. Spain–Queens–Biography. 4. Biography–Middle
Ages, 500-1500. 5. Calendars. I. Title.
D107.3.P45 1990
941'.00992--dc20
    [B]   0-7096
                                                            CIP

ISBN 0-517-58056-X
10 9 8 7 6 5 4 3 2 1

First American Edition

Contents

Introduction

*T*he consorts of England's Plantagenet kings are among the medieval world's most romantic and intriguing women. Of the 15 queens who reigned over England alongside their husbands, from the middle of the 12th century to the 1480s, 13 were born in France. They brought to their new home not only their territorial possessions, but also the artistic heritage and customs of one of Europe's most civilized countries.

Although most of the marriages were arranged for political reasons, an astonishingly high proportion developed into genuine love matches. Henry III and Eleanor of Provence, Richard II and Anne of Bohemia and Henry IV and Joan of Navarre are examples. Other consorts – Isabella 'the she-wolf of France' and Margaret of Anjou are two – enjoyed less happy marriages but changed the course of English history.

This day book is dedicated to 12 of these outstanding women of the Middle Ages.

Eleanor of Aquitaine

1122–1204

*T*he first of England's Plantagenet queens, Eleanor married Henry of Anjou, later Henry II of England, as her second husband in 1152. She was 32, Henry was 20 and their first son, William, was born four months after their wedding.

The eldest child and heiress of William X, duke of Aquitaine, she married her first husband, Louis VII of France, in 1137 at the age of 15 and bore him two daughters, Marie and Alice. In 1147 she took the cross with her husband at Vézelay and accompanied him to the Holy Land on the Second Crusade.

Beautiful, intelligent and forceful, she has become celebrated as much through legend as through historical fact. That she donned the dress of an Amazon and surrounded herself with a band of Amazonian bodyguards is almost certainly invention. That she flirted (and possibly more) with her uncle, Raymond of Antioch, while in Palestine is hinted at by contemporary chroniclers, as is

the unsubstantiated rumour of her affair with Saladin, commander of the Muslim forces in the Third Crusade (who would have been only 11 at the time). Whatever the reason, her marriage to the French king was annulled in 1151.

Eleanor was actively involved with Henry in the political life of England and his French domains, and bore him five sons and three daughters. But relations between king and queen deteriorated. Eleanor's resentment against her husband grew, fuelled by her discovery of his affair with 'The Fair Rosamund' (whom she is rumoured to have bled to death). From 1169 onwards she conspired actively with her sons against their father, even disguising herself as a man to follow her sons to France.

Her influence on the artistic, literary and cultural life of the 12th century was as great as her impact on its politics: she founded her own literary court and under her patronage the medieval tradition of courtly love first emerged. Eleanor died at Fontrevault in France in 1202, at the exceptional age of 82.

JANUARY

1

2

3

4

5

6

7

JANUARY

8

9

10

11

12

13

14

JANUARY

15

16

17

18

19

20

21

JANUARY

22

23

24

25

26

27

28

JANUARY

	29
	30
	31

Berengaria of Navarre

c.1180–1246

*D*aughter of Sancho VI of Navarre, Berengaria was 26 years old when she married Richard I of England, the Lionheart. A close friend of her brother, 'the gallant Sancho', Richard rejected Alice, sister of Philip II of France, to whom he had been betrothed for 20 years, for Berengaria – possibly as much to make an ally of Navarre against France as for love: Berengaria was generally agreed to be more prudent than she was beautiful. Nevertheless, the couple had much in common – Richard, of all the young Plantagenets, shared the Navarre family's love of the arts of music and poetry.

A Provençale princess by birth, and Spanish by descent, Berengaria married the English king in the far-off island of Cyprus, en route to the Holy Land.

Berengaria, chaperoned by Eleanor of Aquitaine, had earlier joined her future husband in Sicily, but because it was Lent, when

marriages could not take place, Richard decided to sail on, with his betrothed, to Palestine – a decision that resulted in Berengaria's capture, after a narrow escape from shipwreck, by Isaac Comnemus, king of Cyprus. Richard's reaction was to attack Comnenus and conquer the island; on her marriage to Richard at Limassol, Berengaria became queen of both Cyprus and England.

In the Holy Land Berengaria lived in harem-like seclusion, her closest companion being Joanna, Richard's sister, during her husband's campaigns against the Saracens. After her return to France, and during Richard's two-year imprisonment at the hands of the Holy Roman Emperor, Henry VI, she lived at Poitou – possibly estranged from her husband who returned to England and abandoned himself 'to drinking and great infamy'.

Berengaria remained devoted to her husband and was probably with him at Chaluz when he was mortally wounded by an arrow shot by a lone crossbowman. After his death she retired to Le Mans; in 1230 she founded the abbey of l'Epau where she died soon afterwards, aged 70.

Berengaria's husband Richard Coeur de Lion

FEBRUARY

1

2

3

4

5

6

7

FEBRUARY

8

9

10

11

12

13

14

FEBRUARY

15

16

17

18

19

20

21

FEBRUARY

22

23

24

25

26

27

28/29

Eleanor
of
Provence

1222–91

*E*leanor of Provence, wife of Henry III of England, was probably one of the country's most unpopular queen consorts. The daughter of Raymond Berengar, count of Provence, she was beautiful, precocious, gifted – before she reached her teens she had composed a heroic poem in the Provençal language – and behaved like a spoilt child.

The marriage was politically advantageous to the English king; Eleanor's sister Margaret was married to Louis IX ('St Louis') of France, creating a link of kinship between the two countries. It was also happy.

Henry, in his late 20s, had rushed to meet his 13-year-old bride at Canterbury, and married her there before taking her to London for her coronation – a sumptuous ceremony at which the royal couple wore glorious jewels and robes lined with ermine. After their marriage he rebuilt his palaces to provide her with chambers

Eleanor and Henry sailing

and chapels, and showered her with expensive presents. When a would-be assassin entered the king's bedchamber in 1238, two years after the wedding, he found it empty: Henry was sleeping in the queen's chamber – behaviour that was almost unheard of at that time.

The court and public, however, soon grew to resent the queen. Extraordinarily extravagant, she was also strongwilled and more determined than her husband. With the Savoyard relatives she brought with her to England she came to play a major role in Plantagenet politics. According to a comtemporary proverb, no one but a Provençal or Poitevin had any hope of advancement.

Eleanor took the veil in 1272 after Henry's death and retired to a nunnery in Amesbury where she died, in 1291, at the age of 70. After the death her son, Edward I was forced to pay off her continuing debts.

MARCH

1

2

3

4

5

6

7

MARCH

8

9

10

11

12

13

14

MARCH

15

16

17

18

19

20

21

MARCH

22

23

24

25

26

27

28

MARCH

	29
	30
	31

Eleanor of Castile

1346–90

*D*aughter of Ferdinand III of Castile and Joanna of Ponthieu, Eleanor, queen of Edward I of England, was loved and admired as a 'model of feminine beauty, combining loveliness, virtue and sweet temper'.

A child bride, she was ten years old when she married Edward at Las Heulgas (he was 15) and it was 18 years before his accession to the English throne made her queen of England. A devoted wife, she enjoyed an unusually happy marriage and accompanied her husband on his travels in France and Spain as well as England. She was with him on crusade in the Holy Land when he was wounded by a Moslem assassin's poisoned dagger: some writers say she sucked the venom from his wound. Others, more realistically, record that she wailed so loudly that the surgeons ordered her from the room.

Eleanor bore Edward 16 children, only six of whom survived to *adulthood. The youngest, the future Edward II, was proclaimed prince of Wales when he was only a few weeks old – at Caernarvon Castle, one of two royal residences in Wales; his mother built a garden within its walls for her family to enjoy.*

Four of her five remaining children – all daughters – died in their thirties or forties, and only one of them, Mary, a nun, lived to be as old as her mother.

Eleanor was travelling with Edward to Scotland when she died suddenly in 1290 at Harby in Lincolnshire, of 'autumnal fever'. She was 47. Devastated by his wife's death, Edward marked the 12 stages of her final journey to Westminster with 12 monumental crosses – the Eleanor Crosses.

Eleanor Cross at Geddington in Northamptonshire

APRIL

1

2

3

4

5

6

7

APRIL

8

9

10

11

12

13

14

APRIL

15

16

17

18

19

20

21

APRIL

22

23

24

25

26

27

28

APRIL

29

30

Isabella of France

1292–1358

*B*orn in 1295 to Philip the Fair of France, from whom she inherited her strikingly good looks, Isabella, 'the she-wolf of France', played a momentous role in English history. She came to England in 1308 as the young bride of Edward II, but despite her beauty, her husband neglected her for his favourite, Piers Gaveston, to whom he gave Isabella's best jewels, wedding presents she had brought with her from France.

When the barons, who resented Gaveston's domination over the king, engineered his execution in 1312, Isabella became closer to her husband and the future Edward III was born later that year. In 1313, she was instrumental in effecting a reconciliation between Edward and his barons. Early in the 1320s, however, the king, on the advice of the Despensers, father and son, who had succeeded Gaveston in his affections, deprived his wife of her estates and her French servants.

In 1325 Isabella was sent to negotiate a treaty with her brother, Charles IV of France. Here she formed first a political and then an amorous liaison with Roger Mortimer, an Englishman exiled in France.

Isabella persuaded her lover and other powerful English barons to join her cause and in 1326 they invaded England. Within four months Edward had been deposed and imprisoned in Berkeley Castle; he died less than a year later, probably at the instigation of Isabella and Mortimer.

The 'she-wolf' and her lover virtually ruled England for three years after Edward III's coronation in 1327. But in 1330 the young king executed Mortimer and retired his mother from public life. Then only 36 years old, she spent the next 28 years at Castle Rising, until her death in 1358 at the age of 63.

MAY

1

2

3

4

5

6

7

MAY

8

9

10

11

12

13

14

MAY

15

16

17

18

19

20

21

MAY

22

23

24

25

26

27

28

MAY

29

30

31

Anne
of
Bohemia

1366–1394

*R*ichard II of England's gentle queen was the eldest daughter of Charles of Luxembourg, king of Bohemia (later Holy Roman Emperor Charles IV) and granddaughter of the blind John of Luxembourg who died fighting for the French at the battle of Crécy.

The couple, both 15 years of age, were married in the newly built St Stephen's Chapel at Westminster in 1382; although the marriage was arranged for political reasons, to enhance the English king's anti-French alliances, Richard was devoted to his wife throughout their 12 years together. Anne, for her part, brought stability to her husband's life and was a moderating influence during the many crises of his reign.

Although English suspicions were at first aroused by the Bohemian followers the new queen brought with her from Prague, they soon grew to appreciate her gentleness and constancy.

Anne's only political blunder was to intervene on behalf of one of her Bohemian ladies-in-waiting, the mistress of Robert de Vere, earl of Oxford: her petition to the pope to sanction de Vere's divorce from his first wife, the king's first cousin, aroused hostility at court.

In 1394 she died of the plague, at the tragically young age of 27. Richard, heartbroken, razed the manor of Sheen, which he had built for his wife, to the ground; and commissioned a joint tomb for himself and Anne. Their effigies, now damaged, originally clasped hands in an expression of eternal love.

Anne on her deathbed surrounded by grieving servants

JUNE

1

2

3

4

5

6

7

JUNE

8

9

10

11

12

13

14

JUNE

15

16

17

18

19

20

21

JUNE

22

23

24

25

26

27

28

JUNE

28

29

30

Isabella
of
Valois

1389–1409

*I*sabella of Valois was six years old when her father, Charles VI of France, eager to secure peace with England, arranged for her to marry Richard II after Anne of Bohemia's death. There was a possibility that the English king might have chosen a Spanish wife and to prevent this Charles suggested three adult brides before offering Isabella, his eldest daughter.

She brought with her £50,000, part of a large dowry, but the bride's age as much as her nationality made the match unpopular in England.

Isabella adored her husband, and Richard himself grew deeply attached to the child, who was left in the care of a French governess, Lady de Coucy, and other French servants. Charles VI's court, scene of the little queen's early childhood, was cultured, pleasure-seeking and extravagant – Richard spent £200,000 to maintain his prestige when he went to France to fetch his bride –

and the habit of extravagance remained with Isabella's French retinue. The king was finally forced to dismiss Lady de Coucy and his wife continued her education under the widowed countess of Hereford.

Isabella was ten years old when Richard died. Devastated by his death – she was ill for two weeks when the news reached her – she remained loyal to his memory. Despite attempts by Henry IV, Richard's successor, to marry her to his son (the future Henry V) and so avoid giving her dowry and jewels back to France, she flatly refused to countenance the match. She was finally allowed to return home after two lonely years of widowhood – at a cost to the English of £4,000.

In 1406 Isabella married her cousin Charles, the poet duke of Orleans, who was four years her junior. She died three years later giving birth to her first child, a daughter, at the age of 19.

JULY

1

2

3

4

5

6

7

Richard II, who married Isabella when she was six years old (Above left)

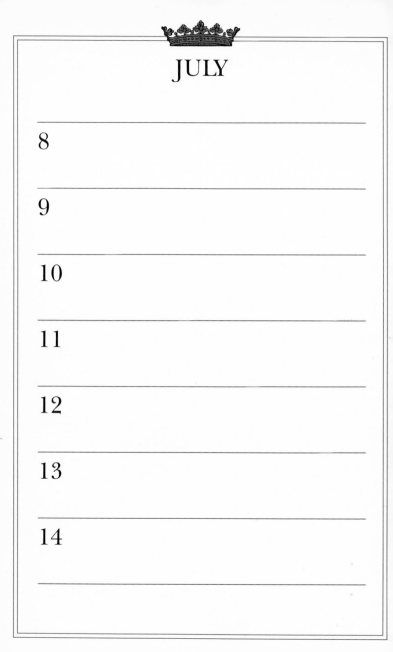

JULY

8

9

10

11

12

13

14

JULY

15

16

17

18

19

20

21

JULY

22

23

24

25

26

27

28

JULY

29

30

31

Joan of Navarre

1370–1437

*J*oan, or Joanna, of Navarre was the widow of John V, duke of Brittany, when, in 1402, she married Henry IV of England, 'the usurper', who in 1399 had deposed his cousin Richard II.

Henry, too, had been married before – his first wife, Mary de Bohun, died in 1394 after bearing him five sons and two daughters – and, unusually, Joan was his personal, rather than political, choice as queen. Ties between the English and Breton ruling families were close and Henry, who met Joan while he was in exile, banished by Richard II, gave her a forget-me-not when he left France to seize the English throne.

The couple were married by proxy in 1402, and in person at Winchester in 1403. Although the marriage was a success, Joan was never popular with the English people. Avarice was her besetting sin. She had inherited a large sum of money from her first husband, and also had the income from her Breton lands;

Joan's coronation as queen following her marriage to Henry IV

nevertheless, she never missed an opportunity to add to her personal wealth.

After Henry's death in 1413 she continued to preside over Henry V's court; her stepson, in his turn, treated her with respect and honour. However, in 1419, when Henry was in France, Joan was arrested by his brother John, duke of Bedford, and charged with the crime of witchcraft: her confessor, John Randolph, accused her of attempting 'the death and destruction' of the king.

Few people at court believed in the accusation – her real 'crime' was to be a drain on the crown's financial resources while England was at war with France – and after an initial imprisonment at Pevensey, she lived in comfort and prosperity until her death, at the age of 67. She was interred in Canterbury Cathedral, in the same vault as Henry IV.

AUGUST

1

2

3

4

5

6

7

AUGUST

8

9

10

11

12

13

14

AUGUST

15

16

17

18

19

20

21

AUGUST

22

23

24

25

26

27

28

AUGUST

29

30

31

Catherine
of
Valois

1401–37

*W*hen Henry V, England's bachelor king, met Catherine of Valois, youngest daughter of the mad French king, Charles VI, in 1419, it was love at first sight; within months, the couple were married in Troyes Cathedral. A contemporary writer describes how, during the wedding night, a procession 'came to the bedside of the royal pair, bringing them wine and soup'. Immediately after the marriage, Henry besieged and won the city of Sens.

Eight months later, in 1421, Catherine made a state entry into London, where the archbishop of Canterbury crowned her queen of England. The future Henry VI was born the following December.

Catherine was very beautiful, but she had neither the intelligence nor the personality to captivate Henry for long. She returned to her parents' home at Senlis early in 1422, and was

Catherine's husband Henry receiving a gift

with them when Henry died. The king, even on his deathbed, made no attempt to send for his young wife.

A widow at 21, Catherine accompanied her husband's body back to England and, for the next eight years, remained there as queen dowager. In 1429 she secretly married Owen Tudor, a Welsh squire; according to tradition, he first came to her attention when, worse the wear for drink, he fell into her lap at a ball. Their grandson, Henry Tudor, became Henry VII of England.

Towards the end of her life, Catherine withdrew to Bermondsey Abbey; she had suffered for many years from what she herself described as a 'grievous malady' – possibly a mental illness inherited from her father Charles VI. She was 36 when she died and was buried, as Henry V's widow, in Westminster Abbey.

SEPTEMBER

1

2

3

4

5

6

7

SEPTEMBER

8

9

10

11

12

13

14

SEPTEMBER

15

16

17

18

19

20

21

SEPTEMBER

22

23

24

25

26

27

28

SEPTEMBER

29

30

Margaret of Anjou

1430–82

*M*argaret of Anjou, Henry VI's strongwilled and forceful queen, played a pivotal role in English history. Daughter of René, duke of Anjou, and, through her mother, a descendant of Charlemagne, her marriage to the English king was a symbol of peace between England and France.

Although she had no dowry, her family was rich in titles and talents, and Margaret, 16 when she married Henry, was as learned as she was beautiful.

She was soon embroiled in court politics, aligning herself with factions opposed to Richard, duke of York, heir presumptive to the English throne during the first childless years of her marriage.

Margaret gave birth to Edward in 1453. By then Henry, already suffering from the mental illness that was to plague him for the rest of his life, was unable to recognise his heir, and Richard had been appointed protector during the king's illness.

When Henry recovered in 1454 the queen persuaded him to dismiss her old enemy from his post, an action that precipitated the battle of St Albans in 1455, the first engagement in the Wars of the Roses between Henry's house of Lancaster and the Yorkists.

For the next 15 years Margaret was in constant conflict with the house of York, continuing her struggle from Scotland and later from France. She returned to England early in 1471 but was defeated and captured at the battle of Tewkesbury; Edward, her son, was killed on the battlefield and Henry was put to death within weeks.

Margaret was imprisoned at Wallingford in Berkshire until 1475 when her cousin, Louis XI of France, ransomed her for £10,000 on condition that she renounced her title and dower rights in England. She retired to Saumur in Anjou where she lived in isolation and poverty until her death, at the age of 52, in 1482.

Margaret of Anjou as she was seen by her subjects

OCTOBER

1st day of journal

1. I can separate better - adequate E.
I planned my life - I love the
ORDER, I am happy - beauty peace +
harmony

2. also want sex & companionship
beware of E surges followed by
a vacume; slow E so can evenly
distribute

3. Every moment is forever

4. Putting things off leads to binges
Eating + TV are avoidance be-
haviors; find out what you
are avoiding + go do it. ♡

5. Nothing day. Nothing to say.
Ate decently, rode bike, watched
TV

6. Lost 2.5 lbs Hurrah! spent
day w/ Dad

7. phone calls - book reading -
CT planning - a play day

↑ 8 a productive happy day, roofers came, art work, truck repair + folk for dinner. Jonathan born — joy!

− 9 discarded another ½ lb. — yea. You have to be yourself to have your dream; destroy your self destroy the dream, ~~loose you loose the dream it~~

↑ 10 ~~happens every time~~ discarded

− total 4 lbs. Going to try dating again. Scary. Don't, won't loose self

↑ 11 dropped off another pound — I can do it + its not all that hard either, now that I'm ready. E surge don't jump ahead nor do nothing try for

− 12 steady flow | Gregg — E + motivation workshop. Have finally accepted that I inherently have alot of E. Now — how to handle it. 1st

↑ 13 MUST get body in shape | Renn Faire - artisans, merchants seem to have most fun. Court to stiff, knights too rowdy. True? ~~Is this who I am?~~

↑ 14 sick |

OCTOBER

sick   15

sick   16

17

18

19

20

21

OCTOBER

22

23

24

25

26

27

28

OCTOBER

29

30

31

Elizabeth Woodville

1437–92

*E*lizabeth Woodville was a widow with two sons when she secretly married Edward IV of England, five years her junior and Europe's most eligible bachelor, in 1464. The match caused consternation in court circles: what would have been a politically advantageous marriage to the niece of Louis XI of France had just been negotiated, and it was in any case impolitic for a monarch to marry one of his subjects. Edward's contemporaries believed that Elizabeth had entrapped the king, a notoriously successful philanderer, by declaring that a wedding ring was the price of her favours.

Elizabeth was beautiful and possibly virtuous. She was also ambitious, arrogant, greedy – and brought with her to court five brothers, seven unmarried sisters and the two sons of her first marriage. Her sisters' advantageous marriages angered established courtiers who themselves had daughters to provide for,

and the family as a whole was widely resented for its influence on the king.

The queen bore Edward three sons and seven daughters. The future Edward V (who was king for only two months) was born in 1470 when his father was in exile and Elizabeth herself in sanctuary in Westminster Abbey, where she remained unharmed until her husband returned triumphant in 1471.

When the king died in 1483 Elizabeth took sanctuary once again in the abbey, but was persuaded to allow her second son, Richard, duke of York, to attend what was said to be Edward V's coronation. Richard of Gloucester, her brother-in-law and the future Richard III, placed both boys in the Tower of London where they were later murdered. He later declared Elizabeth's marriage invalid, and all her children bastards – but gave her a generous pension until she died in 1492.

NOVEMBER

1

2

3

4

5

6

7

NOVEMBER

8

9

10

11

12

13

14

NOVEMBER

15

16

17

18

19

20

21

NOVEMBER

22

23

24

25

26

27

28

NOVEMBER

29

30

Anne Neville

1456–85

*T*he last of the Plantagenet queens, Anne Neville, wife of
Richard III of England, was one of two daughters of
Richard Neville, 'the Kingmaker', 16th earl of Warwick. Like
her elder sister Isabel she was one of the greatest heiresses of the
15th century. Anne was just five years old when her father started
to look for a suitable husband for her, and in 1470 at the age of 14
she was married to Henry VI's only son, the 17-year-old Edward,
prince of Wales. A year later she was widowed when her young
husband was killed at the battle of Tewkesbury.

Anne's sister Isabel married George, duke of Clarence, who,
when his younger brother Richard of Gloucester (later Richard
III) started to show an interest in the young widow (and her
inheritance), concealed Anne in London, disguised as a kitchen
maid: Clarence hoped to retain all the Warwick inheritance in his
wife's right.

Richard found Anne and married her early in 1472, strengthening his claim on traditional Neville loyalties. Her share of her family's estates was absorbed by the crown.

Anne bore only one child – a son, Edward, who was created prince of Wales early in 1483, the year of his parents' coronation. Always frail, he died a year later at the age of 11. The king and queen were 'bordering on madness' in their grief and Anne herself died a year later, aged 29.

Many writers accused Richard of poisoning his young wife in order to marry his niece, Elizabeth of York. The truth is less sensational, but as poignant. Anne died of a wasting disease – probably tuberculosis – which had already killed her sister Isabel.

Anne's husband Richard III

DECEMBER

1

2

3

4

5

6

7

DECEMBER

8

9

10

11

12

13

14

DECEMBER

15

16

17

18

19

20

21

DECEMBER

22

23

24

25

26

27

28

DECEMBER

29

30

31

Bibliography

Bagley, J.J., *Margaret of Anjou, Queen of England*, London, 1948.

Baker, D. ed, *Medieval Women*, Oxford, 1978.

Barber, R.W., *The Knight and Chivalry*, London, 1970.

Barber, R., *The Knight and Chivalry*, London, 1970.

Bennett, H.S., *Life on the English Manor*, Cambridge, 1958.

Clanchy, M.T., *England and its Rulers, 1066–1272*, London, 1983.

Dunbabin, J., *France in the Making, 843–1100*, Oxford, 1985.

Evans, J., *A History of Jewellery, 1100–1870*, London, 1953.

Fawtier, R., *The Capetian Kings of France, Monarchy and Nation, 987–1328*, London, 1966.

Fowler, K.A., *The Age of Plantagenet and Valois*, London, 1967.

Gillingham, J., *Richard the Lionheart*, London, 1978.

Hall, H., *Court Life under the Plantagenets*, London, 1890.

Heltzel, V.B., *Fair Rosamund; the Study of the Development of a Literary Theme*, Evanstown, 1947.

Harvey, J.H., *The Plantagenets*, London, 1948.

Keen, M., *Chivalry*, Yale, 1984.

Keen, M., *England in the Later Middle Ages*, London, 1973.

Kelly, A., *Eleanor of Aquitaine and her Court of Love*, London, 1952.

Kibler, W.W., *Eleanor of Aquitaine, Patron, and Politician*, Austin, 1977.

Lander, J.R., *Crown and Nobility 1405–1509*, London, 1976.

Lewis, P.S., *Later Medieval France*, London, 1968.

Lucas, A., *Medieval Women*, Brighton, 1983.

Bibliography

McFarlane, K.B., *The Nobility of Later Medieval England*, Oxford, 1973.

Ormrod, W.M., *England in the Fourteenth Century*, Woodbridge, 1986.

Pernoud, R., *Eleanor of Aquitaine*, London, 1967.

Poole, A.L., *Medieval England*, Oxford, 1958.

Rene d'Anjou, *Le Cuer d'Amours Espris*, Paris, 1980.

Reuter, T. ed. and trans., *The Medieval Nobility*, Amsterdam, New York, London 1979.

Power, E., *Medieval Women*, Cambridge, 1975.

Pullar, P., *Consuming Passions*, 2nd edn, London, 1972.

Powicke, F.M., *The Thirteenth Century, 1216–1307*, 2nd ed., Oxford, 1962.

Shakar, S., *The Fourth Estate: A History of Women in the Middle Ages*, London, 1983.

Schramm, P.E., *A History of the English Coronation*, Oxford, 1937.

Stenton, D.M., *English Society in Early Middle Ages*, London, 1951.

Thorpe, L., *The History of the Kings of Britain by Geoffrey of Monmouth*, Harmandsworth, 1966.

Topsfield, L.T., *Troubadours and Love*, Cambridge, London, New York, 1975.

Vale, M., *War and Chivalry*, London, 1981.

Warner, M., Joan of Arc, *The Image of Female Heroism*, New York, 1981.

Wilson, C.A., *Food and Drink in Britain*, Harmandsworth, 1984.

Picture Credits

Picture Credits

Anne of Bohemia: Marianne Majerus.
Overleaf: Harley Ms. 4380, fol. 22, British Museum, London.

Isabella of Valois: British Library, London.
Overleaf: British Library, London.

Joane of Navarre: British Library, London.
Overleaf: British Library: Ms. Cott. 6, fol. 2v.

Catherine of Valois: Bibliotheque Nationale, Paris.
Overleaf: Ms. 8/8373, fol. 37, British Library, London.

Elizabeth Woodville: Northampton Art Gallery.
Overleaf: Royal Ms 15, fol. 14, British Library, London.
(Ph: Bridgeman).

Anne Neville: British Library, London.
Overleaf: National Portrait Gallery, London.